Angels in Our Life - How to Contact Them and Live in Harmony with the Universe

Self-Knowledge and Spiritual Development, Volume 1

Ana Mafalda Damião

Published by Ana Mafalda Damião, 2024.

While every precaution has been taken in the preparation of this book, the publisher assumes no responsibility for errors or omissions, or for damages resulting from the use of the information contained herein.

ANGELS IN OUR LIFE - HOW TO CONTACT THEM AND LIVE IN HARMONY WITH THE UNIVERSE

First edition. March 9, 2024.

Copyright © 2024 Ana Mafalda Damião.

ISBN: 979-8224252336

Written by Ana Mafalda Damião.

Also by Ana Mafalda Damião

Aventuras para crianças
Paco: Uma Aventura de Coração

Desenvolvimento Pessoal e Espiritual
Meditação Kind/mindfulness: Programa de 84 dias para mudar a sua vida

Self-awareness
Therapeutic Writing - the Power of Writing in Personal Transformation

Self-Knowledge and Spiritual Development
Angels in Our Life - How to Contact Them and Live in Harmony with the Universe

Standalone
Escrita Terapêutica - o poder da escrita na transformação pessoal
Escrever...o quê? 20 + 8 ideias criativas

Escribir... 20 + 8 Ideas Creativas
Anjos na nossa vida - como contactá-los e viver em sintonia com o universo
Oráculo Das Bruxas
Símbolos E Imagens Para Prever O Futuro
Cristalomancia - A Arte Da Adivinhação Com Cristais
Dominomancia - A Arte Da Adivinhação Com O Dominó
Petit Lenormand - Como Interpretar
Oráculo Dos Druidas
O Poder de Saint Germain
Rituais de conexão - Deusas celtas
Connection Rituals – Celtic Goddesses
The Power of Saint Germain
Ten Plagues of Egypt

Life is a true miracle. Being here and now is a blessing for which we should feel grateful. Every day, in every moment, we can choose to live a magical life. For this, we only need to look around us and see the beauty and love; believe that this is a magical day and feel that it is a gift to be here. The decision to live, or not, in the energy of love is within us. We can choose to feel love for all forms of life; feel respect for the Earth that sustains us and feel united with the Angels that watch over us. And each of our actions can thus be a magical act.

Ana Mafalda Damião

Introduction

When we are born, God sends an angel to Earth with the mission to take care of us throughout our lives. Our guardian angel is with us at all moments; shares our joys and sorrows, concerns and dreams; guides us in confusing times and protects us from less good things; watches over us while we sleep and leads our steps when we are awake. We are a divine spark, a light on Earth, and we came into the world to be happy, to love and be loved. On this path of love, our angel looks after us.

Angelical Hierarchy

The scholars of Kabbalah (the esoteric tradition of the Hebrews) unfolded the name of God – JEHOVAH and added to it the divine names IAH, EL, AEL, IEL to create the names of the 72 guardian angels with these unfoldings and endings. Each guardian angel influences 5 days of our calendar, making up 360 days. There were 5 days left to complete the year, and the Kabbalists dedicated these dates to the angels or geniuses of humanity. All angels are integrated into a hierarchy that is formed by 3 orders, and each order is comprised of 3 choirs. The choirs are led by a prince who governs 8 angels.

First Order – Controls the universal balance and the manifestation of God's will. The three choirs of this order are:

1 – Seraphim – The highest angelic choir. The Seraphim are known as the angels of love. Prince: Metatron Angels: 1 to 8

2 – Cherubim – These angels are tasked with guarding the sacred records and revealing the power and glory of God. Prince: Haziel Angels: 9 to 16

3 – Thrones – Their mission is to inspire faith in God's power in the hearts of men. Prince: Tsaphkiel Angels: 17 to 24

Second Order – Represents the power of God and is tasked with governing the planets, especially Earth. Executes the orders of the first-order angels and directs those of the third order. The three choirs of this order are:

1 – Dominations – Their mission is to maintain order in the cosmos and assist in emergencies. Prince: Tsadkiel Angels: 25 to 32

2 – Powers or Authorities – Their mission is to guard and defend the order in Heaven and prevent evil angels from destroying the world. Prince: Camael Angels: 33 to 40

3 – Virtues – Take care of the movement of planets, stars, and galaxies and control cosmic laws. Protect nature and guide karmic missions. Prince: Raphael Angels: 41 to 48

Third Order – Guides and protects humanity and elevates our prayers to God. The three choirs of this order are:

1 - Principalities – Protect Earth's rulers, enlightening them so their acts are just. Prince: Haniel Angels: 49 to 56

2 – Archangels – Protect the world, fighting against Satan and his legions. Transmit important messages and ensure wisdom and good relationships. Prince: Michael Angels: 57 to 64

3 – Angels – They are the intermediaries between God and men. Prince: Gabriel Angels: 65 to 72

72 Kabbalistic Angels

In the following pages, with your date of birth, you can confirm who your guardian angel is, the order they belong to, and the prince who leads it.

No. 1 – Angel Vehuiah Order - Seraphim Prince - Metatron Birthdates - 20/03, 01/06, 13/08, 25/10, 06/01

No. 2 – Angel Jeliel Order - Seraphim Prince – Metatron Birthdates - 21/03, 02/06, 14/08, 26/10, 07/01

No. 3 – Angel Sitael Order – Seraphim Prince – Metatron Birthdates - 22/03, 03/06, 15/08, 27/10, 08/01

No. 4 – Angel Elemiah Order – Seraphim Prince – Metatron Birthdates - 23/03, 04/06, 16/08, 28/10,09/01

No. 5 – Angel Mahasiah Order – Seraphim Prince – Metatron Birthdates - 24/03, 05/06, 17/08, 29/10,10/01

No. 6 – Angel Lelahel Order – Seraphim Prince – Metatron Birthdates - 25/03, 06/06, 18/08, 30/10, 11/01

No. 7 – Angel Achaiah Order – Seraphim Prince – Metatron Birthdates - 26/03, 07/06, 19/08, 31/10, 12/01

No. 8 – Angel Cahethel Order – Seraphim Prince – Metatron Birthdates - 27/03, 08/06, 20/08, 01/11, 13/01

No. 9 – Angel Haziel Order – Cherubim Prince – Haziel Birthdates - 28/03, 09/06, 21/08, 02/11, 14/01

No. 10 – Angel Aladiah Order – Cherubim Prince – Haziel Birthdates - 29/03, 10/06, 22/08, 03/11, 15/01

No. 11 – Angel Laoviah Order – Cherubim Prince – Haziel Birthdates - 30/03, 11/06, 23/08, 04/11, 16/01

No. 12 – Angel Hahahiah Order – Cherubim Prince – Haziel Birthdates - 31/03, 12/06, 24/08, 05/11, 17/01

No. 13 – Angel Yesalel Order – Cherubim Prince – Haziel Birthdates - 01/04, 13/06, 25/08, 06/11, 18/01

No. 14 – Angel Mebahel Order – Cherubim Prince – Haziel Birthdates - 02/04, 14/06, 26/08, 07/11, 19/01

No. 15 – Angel Hariel Order – Cherubim Prince – Haziel
Birthdates - 03/04, 15/06, 27/08, 08/11, 20/01

No. 16 – Angel Hekamiah Order – Cherubim Prince – Haziel
Birthdates - 04/04, 16/06, 28/08, 09/11, 21/01

No. 17 – Angel Lauviah Order – Thrones Prince – Tsaphkiel
Birthdates - 05/04, 17/06, 29/08, 10/11, 22/01

No. 18 – Angel Caliel Order – Thrones Prince – Tsaphkiel
Birthdates - 06/04, 18/06, 30/08, 11/11, 23/01

No. 19 – Angel Leuviah Order – Thrones Prince – Tsaphkiel
Birthdates - 07/04, 19/06, 31/08, 12/11, 24/01

No. 20 – Angel Pahaliah Order – Thrones Prince – Tsaphkiel
Birthdates - 08/04, 20/06, 01/09, 13/11, 25/01

No. 21 – Angel Nelchael Order – Thrones Prince – Tsaphkiel
Birthdates - 09/04, 21/06, 02/09, 14/11, 26/01

No. 22 – Angel Ieiaiel Order – Thrones Prince – Tsaphkiel
Birthdates - 10/04, 22/06, 03/09, 15/11, 27/01

No. 23 – Angel Melahel Order – Thrones Prince – Tsaphkiel
Birthdates - 11/04, 23/06, 04/09, 16/11, 28/01

No. 24 – Angel Haheuiah Order – Thrones Prince – Tsaphkiel
Birthdates - 12/04, 24/06, 05/09, 17/11, 29/01

No. 25 – Angel Nith-Haiah Order – Dominations Prince – Tsadkiel
Birthdates - 13/04, 25/06, 06/09, 18/11, 30/01

No. 26 – Angel Haaiah Order – Dominations Prince – Tsadkiel
Birthdates - 14/04, 26/06, 07/09, 19/11, 31/01

No. 27 – Angel Ierathel Order – Dominations Prince – Tsadkiel
Birthdates - 15/04, 27/06, 08/09, 20/11, 01/02

No. 28 – Angel Seheiah Order – Dominations Prince – Tsadkiel
Birthdates - 16/04, 28/06, 09/09, 21/11, 02/02

No. 29 – Angel Reyel Order – Dominations Prince – Tsadkiel
Birthdates - 17/04, 29/06, 10/09, 22/11, 03/02

No. 30 – Angel Omael Order – Dominations Prince – Tsadkiel
Birthdates - 18/04, 30/06, 11/09, 23/11, 04/02

No. 31 – Angel Lecabel Order – Dominations Prince – Tsadkiel
Birthdates - 19/04, 01/07, 12/09, 24/11, 05/02

No. 32 – Angel Vasahiah Order – Dominations Prince – Tsadkiel
Birthdates - 20/04, 02/07, 13/09, 25/11, 06/02

No. 33 – Angel Iehuiah Order – Powers Prince – Camael Birthdates - 21/04, 03/07, 14/09, 26/11, 07/02

No. 34 – Angel Lehahiah Order – Powers Prince – Camael Birthdates - 22/04, 04/07, 15/09, 27/11, 08/02

No. 35 – Angel Chavakiah Order – Powers Prince – Camael Birthdates - 23/04, 05/07, 16/09, 28/11, 09/02

No. 36 – Angel Menadel Order – Powers Prince – Camael Birthdates - 24/04, 06/07, 17/09, 29/11, 10/02

No. 37 – Angel Aniel Order – Powers Prince – Camael Birthdates - 25/04, 07/07, 18/09, 30/11, 11/02

No. 38 – Angel Haamiah Order – Powers Prince – Camael Birthdates - 26/04, 08/07, 19/09, 01/12, 12/02

No. 39 – Angel Rehael Order – Powers Prince – Camael Birthdates - 27/04, 09/07, 20/09, 02/12, 13/02

No. 40 – Angel Ieiazel Order – Powers Prince – Camael Birthdates - 28/04, 10/07, 21/09, 03/12, 14/02

No. 41 – Angel Hahahel Order – Virtues Prince – Raphael Birthdates - 29/04, 11/07, 22/09, 04/12, 15/02

No. 42 – Angel Mikael Order – Virtues Prince – Raphael Birthdates - 30/04, 12/07, 23/09, 05/12, 16/02

No. 43 – Angel Veuliah Order – Virtues Prince – Raphael Birthdates - 01/05, 13/07, 24/09, 06/12, 17/02

No. 44 – Angel Yelaiah Order – Virtues Prince – Raphael Birthdates - 02/05, 14/07, 25/09, 07/12, 18/02

No. 45 – Angel Sealiah Order – Virtues Prince – Raphael Birthdates - 03/05, 15/07, 26/09, 08/12, 19/02

No. 46 – Angel Ariel Order – Virtues Prince – Raphael Birthdates - 04/05, 16/07, 27/09, 09/12, 20/02

No. 47 – Angel Asaliah Order – Virtues Prince – Raphael Birthdates - 05/05, 17/07, 28/09, 10/12, 21/02

No. 48 – Angel Mihael Order – Virtues Prince – Raphael Birthdates - 06/05, 18/07, 29/09, 11/12, 22/02

No. 49 – Angel Vehuel Order – Principalities Prince – Haniel Birthdates - 07/05, 19/07, 30/09, 12/12, 23/02

No. 50 – Angel Daniel Order – Principalities Prince – Haniel Birthdates - 08/05, 20/07, 01/10, 13/12, 24/02

No. 51 – Angel Hahasiah Order – Principalities Prince – Haniel
Birthdates - 09/05, 21/07, 02/10, 14/12, 25/02

No. 52 – Angel Imamaiah Order – Principalities Prince – Haniel
Birthdates - 10/05, 22/07, 03/10, 15/12, 26/02

No. 53 – Angel Nanael Order – Principalities Prince – Haniel
Birthdates - 11/05, 23/07, 04/10, 16/12, 27/02

No. 54 – Angel Nithael Order – Principalities Prince – Haniel Birthdates - 12/05, 24/07, 05/10, 17/12, 28 and 29/02

No. 55 – Angel Mebahiah Order – Principalities Prince – Haniel Birthdates - 13/05, 25/07, 06/10, 18/12, 01/03

No. 56 – Angel Poiel Order – Principalities Prince – Haniel Birthdates - 14/05, 26/07, 07/10, 19/12, 02/03

No. 57 – Angel Nemamiah Order – Archangels Prince – Michael Birthdates - 15/05, 27/07, 08/10, 20/12, 03/03

No. 58 – Angel Ieialel Order – Archangels Prince – Michael Birthdates - 16/05, 28/07, 09/10, 21/12, 04/03

No. 59 – Angel Harahel Order – Archangels Prince – Michael Birthdates - 17/05, 29/07, 10/10, 22/12, 05/03

No. 60 – Angel Mitzrael Order – Archangels Prince – Michael Birthdates - 18/05, 30/07, 11/10, 23/12, 06/03

No. 61 – Angel Umabel Order – Archangels Prince – Michael Birthdates - 19/05, 31/07, 12/10, 24/12, 07/03

No. 62 – Angel Iah-Hel Order – Archangels Prince – Michael Birthdates - 20/05, 01/08, 13/10, 25/12, 08/03

No. 63 – Angel Anauel Order – Archangels Prince – Michael Birthdates - 21/05, 02/08, 14/10, 26/12, 09/03

No. 64 – Angel Mehiel Order – Archangels Prince – Michael Birthdates - 22/05, 03/08, 15/10, 27/12, 10/03

No. 65 – Angel Damabiah Order – Angels Prince – Gabriel Birthdates - 23/05, 04/08, 16/10, 28/12, 11/03

No. 66 – Angel Manakel Order – Angels Prince – Gabriel Birthdates - 24/05, 05/08, 17/10, 29/12, 12/03

No. 67 – Angel Ayel Order – Angels Prince – Gabriel Birthdates - 25/05, 06/08, 18/10, 30/12, 13/03

No. 68 – Angel Habuhiah Order – Angels Prince – Gabriel Birthdates - 26/05, 07/08, 19/10, 31/12, 14/03

No. 69 – Angel Rochel Order – Angels Prince – Gabriel Birthdates - 27/05, 08/08, 20/10, 01/01, 15/03

No. 70 – Angel Yabamiah Order – Angels Prince – Gabriel Birthdates - 28/05, 09/08, 21/10, 02/01, 16/03

No. 71 – Angel Haiaiel Order – Angels Prince – Gabriel Birthdates - 29/05, 10/08, 22/10, 03/01, 17/03

No. 72 – Angel Mumiah Order – Angels Prince – Gabriel Birthdates
- 30/05, 11/08, 23/10, 04/01, 18/03

Angels or Geniuses of Humanity: Those born on January 5, March
19, May 31, August 12, and October 24.

Meaning of the names of angels in Hebrew

1st Angel – Vehuiah – God elevated and exalted above all things
2nd Angel - Jeliel – God who assists
3rd Angel – Sitael – God, the hope of all creatures
4th Angel – Elemiah – Hidden God
5th Angel – Mahasiah – God the Savior
6th Angel – Lelahel – Praiseworthy God
7th Angel – Achaiah – Good and patient God
8th Angel – Cahethel – God of abundance
9th Angel – Haziel – God of mercy
10th Angel Aladiah – Most amiable God
11th Angel – Laoviah – Praised and exalted God
12th Angel – Hahahiah – God of refuge
13th Angel – Yesalel – Glorified God
14th Angel – Mebahel – Preserving God
15th Angel – Hariel – God the Creator
16th Angel – Hekamiah – God constructs the universe
17th Angel – Lauviah – Wonderful God
18th Angel – Caliel – God ready to welcome
19th Angel – Leuviah – God who welcomes sinners
20th Angel – Pahaliah – Redeeming God
21st Angel – Nelchael – Sole and unique God
22nd Angel – Ieiaiel – Just and perfect God
23rd Angel – Melahel – God who delivers us from evil

24th Angel – Haheuiah – Intrinsically good God

25th Angel - Nith-Haiah – God who gives wisdom

26th Angel – Haaiah – Hidden God

27th Angel – Ierathel – God who punishes the wicked

28th Angel – Seheiah – God who heals the sick

29th Angel – Reyel – God ready to assist

30th Angel – Omael – Patient God
31st Angel – Lecabel – Inspiring God
32nd Angel – Vasahiah – Pious God
33rd Angel – Iehuiah – God who knows all things
34th Angel – Lehahiah – Merciful God
35th Angel – Chavakiah – God who gives joy
36th Angel – Menadel – Adorable God
37th Angel – Aniel – God of virtues
38th Angel – Haamiah – Hope of all the earth's children
39th Angel – Rehael – God who welcomes sinners
40th Angel – Ieiazel – God who gives joy
41st Angel – Hahahel – God in three persons
42nd Angel – Mikael – The house of God
43rd Angel – Veuliah – Dominating God
44th Angel – Yelaiah – Eternal God
45th Angel – Sealiah – The mover of all things
46th Angel – Ariel – Revealing God
47th Angel – Asaliah – Just God who points to the truth
48th Angel – Mihael – God the father who assists
49th Angel – Vehuel – Great and elevated God
50th Angel – Daniel – Lord of mercies
51st Angel – Hahasiah – Hidden God
52nd Angel – Imamaiah – God above all things
53rd Angel – Nanael – God who humbles the proud
54th Angel – Nithael – King of heaven
55th Angel – Mebahiah – Eternal God
56th Angel – Poiel – God who supports the universe
57th Angel – Nemamiah – Praiseworthy God
58th Angel – Ieialel – God who welcomes generations
59th Angel – Harahel – God of wisdom
60th Angel – Mitzrael – God who comforts the oppressed

61st Angel – Umabel – God above everything

62nd Angel - Iah-Hel – Supreme Being

63rd Angel – Anauel – Infinitely good God

64th Angel – Mehiel – Life-giving God

65th Angel – Damabiah – God source of wisdom

66th Angel – Manakel – God who supports and maintains everything in the world

67th Angel – Ayel – God delight of children

68th Angel – Habuhiah – God of goodness

69th Angel – Rochel – God who sees everything

70th Angel – Yabamiah – The Word that creates all things

71st Angel – Haiaiel – God master of the universe

72nd Angel – Mumiah – Omega, the end of all

Us and our Guardian Angels

Everyone has a guardian angel, but we also have a contrary spirit who is always trying to tempt us to do fewer good things. This contrary spirit approaches whenever the guardian angel distances themselves. Therefore, we must always maintain close contact with our angel and avoid becoming irritated, impatient, intolerant, viewing life negatively, and so on. Angels are energy, a very light matter, existing on a higher plane. To draw closer to us, into our energy field, our emotions must be light. Anger, wrath, resentment, hatred, sadness, envy... are strong emotions that create dense energy preventing angels from approaching. In each of us, personality traits are closely linked to our guardian angel, and when we let ourselves be enveloped by negativity, we manifest characteristics of the contrary spirit. Knowing these traits is a way to consciously avoid them. Look for your angel in the following pages, and learn about the personality traits directly linked to you.

1st Angel - Vehuiah (20/03, 01/06, 13/08, 25/10, 06/01) Those born under the protection of this angel are very curious and in a constant search for truth. Internally they are balanced, optimistic beings with a great capacity for adaptation. They value friendship and family. They tend to have intense passions, though often short-lived. They reveal great learning capabilities in science and the arts, where they can shine. These beings love social life and have strong magnetism. When the contrary spirit dominates – they become aggressive.

2nd Angel - Jeliel (21/03, 02/06, 14/08, 26/10, 07/01) Those born under this angel's protection are very impatient and tend to do everything too quickly. Long expositions bother them because they always feel like they already know everything. They are very intuitive and instantly recognize the difference between right and wrong. They know they have a mission to fulfill on Earth and experience very strong emotions, condemning violence above all. They reveal a sense of humor that helps them find and maintain many friends throughout life. When the contrary spirit dominates – they become selfish and insensitive.

3rd Angel – Sitael (22/03, 03/06, 15/08, 27/10, 08/01) Those born under Sitael's influence are very fortunate beings, with a great capacity to achieve a high economic level. They are born fighters, not easily giving up on their goals. Due to pride, they find it hard to ask for help even in tough times. Despite this, they live surrounded by friends, loving everything related to social life. They are very cultured beings with a great capacity to forgive. When the contrary spirit dominates – they can become ungrateful people.

4th Angel - Elemiah (23/03, 04/06, 16/08, 28/10, 09/01) Those born under this angel's influence are very mystical beings, who know their true mission on Earth and spend most of their time trying to help others. They have a great capacity for work, dedicating themselves to multiple projects at the same time. They are very envied, which sometimes causes them some sadness. When the contrary spirit dominates – they may turn to vices.

5th Angel – Mahasiah (24/03, 05/06, 17/08, 29/10, 10/01) Those protected by this angel have a great learning capacity because they carry many memories from other incarnations. They are balanced and always act according to the laws. They can dedicate themselves to working with spiritual beings, as their communication with angels is very strong. They like to live comfortably, in large spaces surrounded by books. When the contrary spirit dominates – they take advantage of others' good faith.

6th Angel - Lelahel (25/03, 06/06, 18/08, 30/10, 11/01) Those born under this angel's protection are balanced and idealistic beings. They are very gifted for the arts and can achieve great fortunes, because they were born with an inner light that always leads them to the best path. They are attracted to the unknown and easily, they can contact other dimensions. They are beings with a great capacity to love, making it very easy for them to find love in all the paths they tread. When the contrary spirit dominates – they become ambitious and opportunistic.

7th Angel - Achaiah (26/03, 07/06, 19/08, 31/10, 12/01) Those born under the influence of this angel recognize the existence and importance of spirituality from an early age. They are curious, persistent, and seek truth above all. They are very patient and tolerant. When the contrary spirit dominates – they become negligent and lose the ability to face difficulties.

8th Angel - Cahethel (27/03, 08/06, 20/08, 01/11, 13/01) The protected ones of this angel are balanced people with strong control over their emotions. They always follow their intuition, even if it sometimes makes them misunderstood. They enjoy traveling to experience different cultures. When the contrary spirit dominates – they become proud and contentious.

9th Angel - Haziel (28/03, 09/06, 21/08, 02/11, 14/01) If you were born under the protection of this angel, you tend to do important work, thereby winning everyone's sympathy. You are a person of noble and loyal character. You trust in divine protection and know that in the most difficult moments, you can count on it. You do not fear obstacles because you believe that good will always triumph. You possess an enormous capacity for forgiveness. When the contrary spirit dominates – you become arrogant.

10th Angel - Aladiah (29/03, 10/06, 22/08, 03/11, 15/01) Those born under the protection of this angel will be remembered as beings with open hearts, always ready to practice kindness. They will act as an angel on earth, helping all those who turn to them. Despite having an intense social life, they are reserved and devoted to family. They will always choose the most correct path because they are endowed with great imagination and self-confidence. Their efforts will always aim to contribute to the formation of a fairer society. When the contrary spirit dominates – they become negligent and prone to improper acts.

11th Angel - Laoviah (30/03, 11/06, 23/08, 04/11, 16/01) If born under the protection of this angel, you will become famous for your deeds and will draw from all experiences the knowledge necessary for your growth. Financially, you will easily achieve prosperity. You are endowed with a great capacity to love. When the contrary spirit dominates – you become rude, ambitious, and jealous.

12th Angel - Hahahiah (31/03, 12/06, 24/08, 05/11, 17/01) The protected ones of this angel have a very marked personality; they are intelligent, spiritual, and discreet. Their attitudes towards others are always balanced and governed by tolerance. They are calm and were born with the mission to teach, valuing books as one of the forms of knowledge. Their speech is always in harmony with the universe, and their charisma and beauty ease their affectionate relationships. When the contrary spirit dominates – they become indiscreet.

13th Angel - Yesalel (01/04, 13/06, 25/08, 06/11, 18/01) Those born under the protection of this angel are very intelligent, possessing a great capacity for memory and learning in all areas. They accept life as it is, without complaining or lamenting the lesser things. They always avoid judging others, a capability that comes from their healthy connection with spirituality. Their optimism helps them find friends everywhere they go. When the contrary spirit dominates – they become whimsical.

14th Angel - Mebahel (02/04, 14/06, 26/08, 07/11, 19/01) If born under the protection of this angel, you appreciate the arts and esoteric sciences. You have the ability to work with magic, which you often do as a way to expand your spirituality. You are fair and straightforward in their relationships with others and simplify life as much as possible. They are extremely good-humoured, which makes them very pleasant company. When the contrary spirit dominates – they become very individualistic and intolerant.

15th Angel – Hariel (03/04, 15/06, 27/08, 08/11, 20/01) Those born under the protection of this angel live simply and are always grateful for life. They possess knowledge of esoteric sciences and, through their work, can contribute to the growth of spirituality. Their sense of humor will make the lives of those around them more joyful, and they will make many friends. When the contrary spirit dominates – they become very materialistic.

16th Angel - Hekamiah (04/04, 16/06, 28/08, 09/11, 21/01) The protected ones of this angel are sincere, loyal, and their watchword is peace. They have a strong tendency to help the oppressed, showing unparalleled courage. They become respected people for their frank character and actions. They are very sensual and value physical appearance. They detest routine and are very creative. When the contrary spirit dominates – they become unfaithful.

17th Angel - Lauviah (05/04, 17/06, 29/08, 10/11, 22/01) Those born under the influence of this angel master symbolism, becoming known for their interpretations of it. They can become famous in the fields of music, painting, or writing. All their dreams will come true, but they will always struggle to achieve a comfortable economic situation. When the contrary spirit dominates – they can become deceitful and inspire fear in others.

18th Angel - Caliel (06/04, 18/06, 30/08, 11/11, 23/01) If born under the protection of this angel, you possess a strong personal magnetism and are very intelligent. You dislike vague ideas and strive to master important knowledge in the areas that please you most. You are fair and honest in your relationships with others. When the contrary spirit dominates – you become scheming and prone to creating conflicts.

19th Angel - Leuviah (07/04, 19/06, 31/08, 12/11, 24/01) The protected ones of this angel are very simple and modest beings. They love the arts and may make it their profession. They never get discouraged by life's adversities because they know they are protected and loved by beings of light. They don't let others interfere in their personal life, nor do they interfere in matters that don't concern them directly. They are amiable in their day-to-day relationships. When the contrary spirit dominates – they become too intolerant.

20th Angel - Pahaliah (08/04, 20/06, 01/09, 13/11, 25/01) If born under the protection of this angel, you are a person with a very strong personality who never gives up fighting for what you want. You enjoy being at peace but can't stand being alone. You are a true optimist and always keep smiling, even in the hardest times. When the contrary spirit dominates – you become overbearing.

21st Angel - Nelchael (09/04, 21/06, 02/09, 14/11, 26/01) If under the influence of this angel, you possess great leadership ability, self-control, and infinite patience. A lover of beauty, you cannot stand vulgarity. You love poetry and painting. In relationships, you seek your soulmate and cope well with loneliness if you don't find them. When the contrary spirit dominates – you become aggressive.

22nd Angel - Ieiaiel (10/04, 22/06, 03/09, 15/11, 27/01) People born under the protection of this angel live with a pressing need to travel and discover new things. They are original in their thinking and actions and have a great communication capacity. They possess mediumistic abilities. When the contrary spirit dominates – they become racist.

23rd Angel - Melahel (11/04, 23/06, 04/09, 16/11, 28/01) The protected ones of this angel are very upright people, lovers of order, and fulfillers of their tasks. They express themselves very clearly, especially regarding their feelings. Although they appear reserved at first contact, they easily make friendships that last forever. They defend nature and animals with the same intensity they defend humans. When the contrary spirit dominates – they become liars.

24th Angel - Haheuiah (12/04, 24/06, 05/09, 17/11, 29/01) The protected ones of this angel have a very strong connection with their parents and find it hard to leave home. They are very concerned about the safety of their family and community. They are very intelligent and have an innate capacity for business. Religion may provide them with answers to their doubts. When the contrary spirit dominates – they incite others to violence.

25th Angel - Nith-Haiah (13/04, 25/06, 06/09, 18/11, 30/01) The protected ones of this angel are moderate, serene, balanced, and very patient beings. They love peace, solitude, and contemplation and live in perfect harmony with nature. They do not question the difficulties that come their way. They are very protected by family and friends. When the contrary spirit dominates – they become resentful.

26th Angel - Haaiah (14/04, 26/06, 07/09, 19/11, 31/01) Those born under the protection of this angel are just, balanced, and kind. They appreciate long-lasting relationships. They love to travel, adapting well to all environments. They are very popular. When the contrary spirit dominates – they become overly ambitious.

27th Angel - Ierathel (15/04, 27/06, 08/09, 20/11, 01/02) People born under the protection of this angel are very intelligent and balanced. They cultivate a noble appearance, live joyfully, and have a great capacity for initiative. They never give up on their goals. They are very gifted for divinatory arts and can practice any oracle they like. When the contrary spirit dominates – they become intolerant and violent.

28th Angel - Seheiah (16/04, 28/06, 09/09, 21/11, 02/02) Those born under the protection of this angel are very sensible and will always act with caution and wisdom. They are beings for whom truth is very valuable and who have a great ability to overcome obstacles, thanks to their imaginative capabilities. They possess the power of healing. When the contrary spirit dominates – they become disorganized, and their lives can become chaotic.

29th Angel - Reyel (17/04, 29/06, 10/09, 22/11, 03/02) People protected by this angel are distinguished by their qualities and the desire to spread hope. They live exemplarily, loving peace, silence, and justice. They reveal great spirituality, often expressed through art. When the contrary spirit dominates – they become selfish and hypocritical.

30th Angel - Omael (18/04, 30/06, 11/09, 23/11, 04/02) The protected ones of this angel are just beings, living in perfect harmony with the universe. They possess a good dose of self-confidence, which helps them never give up on their ideals. They know they are protected by their angel, and this is where their inner strength comes from. They are lovers of nature and animals. When the contrary spirit dominates – they become indifferent to everything.

31st Angel - Lecabel (19/04, 01/07, 12/09, 24/11, 05/02) Those born under the influence of this angel are endowed with great courage to face life's adversities. They love to read and tend to delve deep into the topics that please them, especially reincarnation. They fight for the preservation of nature and tend to adopt animals they find abandoned. When the contrary spirit dominates – they become lazy.

32nd Angel - Vasahiah (20/04, 02/07, 13/09, 25/11, 06/02) The protected ones of this angel are amiable and modest in their relationships. They possess a good memory and like to learn other languages. Endowed with a great capacity for communication, they spread the word of their angel everywhere. They never postpone their decisions. When the contrary spirit dominates – they become irresponsible.

33rd Angel - Iehuiah (21/04, 03/07, 14/09, 26/11, 07/02) People born under the influence of this angel are very understanding and friendly, maintaining excellent relations with everyone. They strive to develop their spiritual abilities and courageously fight for their ideals. For their inner balance, they need to live in calm places. When the contrary spirit dominates – they become intolerant and obsessive in the pursuit of material goods.

34th Angel - Lehahiah (22/04, 04/07, 15/09, 27/11, 08/02) The protected ones of this angel are peaceful beings who will become famous for their talents and actions. They defend moral principles, kindness, and hospitality, and their attitudes are always firm. They cannot stand disorder, and for their emotional balance to be maintained, they need to live in calm and organized places. Their paranormal abilities may manifest through telepathy and clairvoyance. When the contrary spirit dominates – they become stubborn and foolish.

35th Angel - Chavakiah (23/04, 05/07, 16/09, 28/11, 09/02) People born under this angel's protection have difficulty understanding and accepting social inequalities. They will always stand by the weaker and less fortunate. They are practical beings who easily solve any issue without complicating life. They are discreet and very pleasant in their relationships with others. When the contrary spirit dominates – they become unpleasant and tend to create conflicts.

36th Angel – Menadel (24/04, 06/07, 17/09, 29/11, 10/02) Those born under the protection of this angel will have an iron will, never giving up on their dreams. They are intelligent and self-confident beings who always approach problems in a direct manner. Their extreme dedication to others often makes them feel unreciprocated. They always expect sincerity, which does not always happen. They may succeed in careers related to communication. When the contrary spirit dominates – they become lazy.

37th Angel – Aniel (25/04, 07/07, 18/09, 30/11, 11/02) Those born under the influence of this angel will be famous for their talents. Their enthusiasm for life is contagious, making them welcome everywhere. They will fight against prejudice and for a fairer society. When the contrary spirit dominates – they become materialistic and tend to disconnect from their family.

38th Angel – Haamiah (26/04, 08/07, 19/09, 01/12, 12/02) People born under the protection of this angel will follow God's principles in all areas of their life. Their knowledge will be acquired through reading. Others can always count on their help and their intuitive ability to solve problems. They are great defenders of individual freedoms, detesting possessiveness. When the contrary spirit dominates – they become fanatical.

39th Angel – Rehael (27/04, 09/07, 20/09, 02/12, 13/02) People born under the protection of this angel have the ability to heal through the laying on of hands, the power of the mind, and positive prayers or thoughts. They tend to participate in all their community's activities as a way to get closer to others. They are very optimistic. When the contrary spirit dominates – they become cruel.

40th Angel – Ieiazel (28/04, 10/07, 21/09, 03/12, 14/02) The protected ones of this angel are very intelligent beings with a great vocation for literature and sciences. Their ideas will always be brilliant, and their thoughts sublime. They are not attached to money, but they will never lack it. They possess a noble character and a strong intuition. They value love above everything. When the contrary spirit dominates – they become pessimistic and neglectful of themselves.

41st Angel – Hahahel (29/04, 11/07, 22/09, 04/12, 15/02) Those born under the protection of this angel are lovers of truth and fulfil their obligations. They know they have a mission on Earth, but struggle with the doubt of not knowing where to start to fulfil their path. They are always surrounded by friends and place the good of others above their own. When the contrary spirit dominates – they tend to despise those they consider below their social level.

42nd Angel – Mikael (30/04, 12/07, 23/09, 05/12, 16/02) People born under the protection of this angel exhibit upright behaviour throughout their lives. They never make hasty decisions, always carefully observing the options that come their way. They are sincere in their relationships, self-confident, and have a good sense of humour. When the contrary spirit dominates – they become selfish.

43rd Angel – Veuliah (01/05, 13/07, 24/09, 06/12, 17/02) People born under the influence of this angel will always display upright behaviour, even in the most complicated situations. They are very hardworking, which contributes to them becoming esteemed in their community. They are cautious and overcome obstacles with good sense and intelligence. They are sincere and altruistic. They do not get lost in internal conflicts and illuminate others with their inexhaustible self-confidence and good humour. When the contrary spirit dominates – they promote discord through intrigue and bad advice.

44th Angel – Yealaiah (02/05, 14/07, 25/09, 07/12, 18/02) The protected ones of this angel love to travel, have much knowledge, and will be successful. They are very secure and hardworking people. They always feel inspired by their angel, who gives them strength to fight for their dreams. When the contrary spirit dominates – they cause discontent wherever they go.

45th Angel – Sealiah (03/05, 15/07, 26/09, 08/12, 19/02) Those born under the protection of this angel are very attached to home and family. They possess the gift of divination, which they may use to help those close to them. This gift can be transmitted through dreams, premonitions, or the use of an oracle. Their actions towards others will increase their connection to the angels. When the contrary spirit dominates – they become unbalanced beings.

46th Angel – Ariel (04/05, 16/07, 27/09, 09/12, 20/02) Those who have this angel as their protector are discreet beings, always endowed with unusual ideas and a strong spirit. They respect all human beings and have a special affection for the elderly. They will triumph in all areas of life. When the contrary spirit dominates – they assume immature attitudes.

47th Angel – Asaliah (05/05, 17/07, 28/09, 10/12, 21/02) People born under the protection of this angel have strong charisma, showing tenderness and gentleness in their relationships. They have a pleasant and dynamic character, engaging in numerous activities. In complicated matters, they act immediately, detesting confusion. They are proud and like to excel in what they do. When the contrary spirit dominates – they become very possessive.

48th Angel – Mihael (06/05, 18/07, 29/09, 11/12, 22/02) The protected ones of this angel are gentle beings, lovers of peace, and great defenders of humanity. They defend all the oppressed and will fight for the rights of all human beings. They may work with children, especially in health, as they are born with a gift for this role. They are very attached to family. When the contrary spirit dominates – they tend to provoke family conflicts.

49th Angel – Vehuel (07/05, 19/07, 30/09, 12/12, 23/02) The protected ones of this angel are very generous people, known for their virtues and communication skills. Their friendship towards others is unlimited, and they do everything to help. Their intellectual gifts and the way they fight for their ideals may lead some to consider them stubborn. They never miss their commitments. When the contrary spirit dominates – they become selfish and vain.

50th Angel – Daniel (08/05, 20/07, 01/10, 13/12, 24/02) People born under the protection of this angel are very patient, accepting others' flaws as a natural thing. They cannot stand injustice, showing themselves to be less tolerant in such cases. They hate dubious situations and never act without thinking. When the contrary spirit dominates – they become distressed.

51st Angel – Hahasiah (09/05, 21/07, 02/10, 14/12, 25/02) Those born under the protection of this angel are very creative and live their lives in harmony. Angelic revelations will be part of their daily lives and guide their steps in helping others. When the contrary spirit dominates – they tend to deceive others for their own benefit.

52nd Angel – Imamaiah (10/05, 22/07, 03/10, 15/12, 26/02) Those who have this angel as their protector possess a strong personality and a great capacity to resist frustration. Instinctive attitudes are unknown to them. They always act based on reason and do not take unnecessary risks. They are intelligent, sentimental, and optimistic. When the contrary spirit dominates – they become proud.

53rd Angel – Nanael (11/05, 23/07, 04/10, 16/12, 27/02) People protected by this angel are very affectionate, and their great goal is for love to be the force that rules the world. They fight for this ideal and lead their lives in peace and harmony with the universal forces. When the contrary spirit dominates – they become sad beings, unable to fight for their dreams.

54th Angel – Nithael (12/05, 24/07, 05/10, 17/12, 28 and 29/02) Those born under the protection of this angel will be famous for their written works and their public speaking skills. They may hold leadership positions because they are fair, orderly, and never act against the laws. They will achieve all the goals they set for themselves. When the contrary spirit dominates – they become unreliable.

55th Angel – Mebahiah (13/05, 25/07, 06/10, 18/12, 01/03) People born under the protection of this angel live simply, without valuing material goods. Despite being elevated beings, they will always be misunderstood. Often, others will think they are false, which will bring them great sadness. They will need to deepen their contacts with beings of Light to overcome these issues. When the contrary spirit dominates – they will act against love.

56th Angel – Poiel (14/05, 26/07, 07/10, 19/12, 02/03) Those born under the protection of this angel are modest and good-humoured, esteemed by all those around them. They believe that only love makes people happy. They are very optimistic. When the contrary spirit dominates – they are overcome by ambition and pride.

57th Angel – Nemamiah (15/05, 27/07, 08/10, 20/12, 03/03) The protected ones of this angel will be distinguished by their leadership abilities and their affection for everything in the universe. They will fight for the right to equality. The angels contact them through dreams, which allows them to guide those around them. When the contrary spirit dominates – they become liars and cowards.

58th Angel – Ieialel (16/05, 28/07, 09/10, 21/12, 04/03) The protected ones of this angel are known for their courage and frankness in relationships. They are people with an affectionate temperament, optimistic and decisive. They do not like taking unnecessary risks. When the contrary spirit dominates – they become vengeful.

59th Angel – Harahel (17/05, 29/07, 10/10, 22/12, 05/03) Those born under the influence of this angel will be intelligent beings, always seeking new knowledge. They will stand out for their charisma, humor, and courage. They will always have the desire to share material goods. These people will have the ability to work with oracles and practice healing. When the contrary spirit dominates – they become unreliable.

60th Angel – Mitzrael (18/05, 30/07, 11/10, 23/12, 06/03) The protected ones of this angel possess many talents which they do not hesitate to put at the service of others. They seek wisdom and balance, spending most of their lives studying. They recognize the divine spark in every being they come across. When the contrary spirit dominates – they become arrogant.

61st Angel – Umabel (19/05, 31/07, 12/10, 24/12, 07/03) People born under the influence of this angel will have a strong sensitivity and love for all forms of life. They love to travel, but sudden changes cause them emotional distress. They have a great capacity for sacrifice, not hesitating to harm themselves to favour their family members. When the contrary spirit dominates – they become very detached from the family.

62nd Angel – Iah-Hel (20/05, 01/08, 13/10, 25/12, 08/03) The protected ones of this angel are calm beings who love simplicity and tranquillity above all. They fulfil their family obligations. They reveal an open spirit and an energy that they can use for personal growth and for the common good. When driven by an ideal, they are perseverant in their attitudes. When the contrary spirit dominates – they live futilely.

63rd Angel – Anauel (21/05, 02/08, 14/10, 26/12, 09/03) Those born under the influence of this angel will stand out for their work and intelligence. These people are endowed with a strong intuition. Material security does not concern them, as they trust in divine strength and know that they will lack nothing. When the contrary spirit dominates – they will use their intelligence to discover others' weaknesses.

64th Angel – Mehiel (22/05, 03/08, 15/10, 27/12, 10/03) The protected ones of this angel aim for knowledge in life. They are affectionate and always find the good side of people. They are very tolerant, which sometimes brings them displeasure. Many may consider them naive and try to take advantage of the goodwill they show. When the contrary spirit dominates – they become vain.

65th Angel – Damabiah (23/05, 04/08, 16/10, 28/12, 11/03) The protected ones of this angel are fortunate beings who will achieve a very advantageous economic position. They live eccentrically, prioritizing adventure above everything. They do not create bonds with the places they live in and feel a constant need for change. Routine stresses them out. When the contrary spirit dominates – they become emotionally unbalanced.

66th Angel – Manakel (24/05, 05/08, 17/10, 29/12, 12/03) People born under the protection of this angel possess many qualities and will become known for their character, friendliness, and kindness. They are very determined and do not know the word discouragement. They will never be afraid to explore unknown paths. They will make many friends throughout life. When the contrary spirit dominates – they become very discouraged and lack the strength to fight for their dreams.

67th Angel – Ayel (25/05, 06/08, 18/10, 30/12, 13/03) People born under the protection of this angel are very attached to their family, from whom they hardly separate. They like to learn and despise trivialities. When the contrary spirit dominates – they become embittered.

68th Angel – Habuhiah (26/05, 07/08, 19/10, 31/12, 14/03) People born under the protection of this angel are noble and altruistic in their relationships. However, they only approach those with whom they share affinities. They may tend to isolate themselves to more intensely feel the forces of the universe. When the contrary spirit dominates – they have great difficulty feeling affection for others.

69th Angel – Rochel (27/05, 08/08, 20/10, 01/01, 15/03) The protected ones of this angel are very intuitive beings and feel the suffering of all those around them. They possess strong energy and a creative spirit, which will help them face all situations, even the most adverse. When the contrary spirit dominates – they become stubborn and selfish.

70th Angel – Yabamiah (28/05, 09/08, 21/10, 02/01, 16/03) People born under the protection of this angel have been graced with the powers of all beings of light. Nothing that happens around them goes unnoticed. When someone needs help, they are the first to take the initiative. Despite being reserved and introspective, their confidence and optimism will make them highly sought-after individuals. When the contrary spirit dominates – they become arrogant.

71st Angel – Haiaiel (29/05, 10/08, 22/10, 03/01, 17/03) Those born under the influence of this angel will fight against all types of injustices because they possess a strong sense of right and wrong. Their behavior will be exemplary, never harming anyone. These people often feel the need to isolate themselves to regain the emotional balance that makes them such special beings. When the contrary spirit dominates – they become envious.

72nd Angel – Mumiah (30/05, 11/08, 23/10, 04/01, 18/03) The protected ones of this angel love change because it forces them to new ways of thinking. They cannot stand sadness and always try to help those who are depressed. Their ideals will command their lives, and they fight for them without ever giving up. When the contrary angel dominates – they become aggressive and sad beings.

Angels of Humanity or Geniuses are all people born on January 5th, March 19th, May 31st, August 12th, and October 24th. They carry the karmic mission of protecting humanity. They are very intelligent and have the ability to control the forces of the elements (earth, air, fire, and water) and the elementals (fairies, gnomes, sylphs, undines, and salamanders). Those born:

- On 01/05 are very patient, communicative, and intelligent. They easily achieve success. They are excellent counsellors because they possess great spiritual clarity and a strong sense of justice.
- On 19/03 have strong magnetism and a perfect awareness of their power. They never forget their fellow beings, with whom they share their wisdom and material goods. They are very organized and love challenges.
- On 31/05 are known for their communication skills and adventurous spirit. They love new experiences, especially those that stimulate their intelligence. They are very active and are always putting into practice the knowledge they acquire.
- On 12/08 are very extroverted and have a strong influence over others. They use their energy in study and discovery. They like to face difficult situations, are proud, and hardworking.
- On 24/10 are very emotional, persistent, and intuitive. They have no difficulty overcoming hard times and are constantly in search of new ideals.

Angelic Gifts

We all receive a gift from each of the 72 angels, and these gifts will assist us throughout life. By knowing the gift each angel offers us, we can develop it through prayers, meditations, and positive thinking.

1st Angel – Vehuiah Gift – curiosity
2nd Angel - Jeliel Gift – harmony
3rd Angel – Sitael Gift - nobility of character
4th Angel – Elemiah Gift – mysticism
5th Angel – Mahasiah Gift – peace
6th Angel – Lelahel Gift – healing
7th Angel – Achaiah Gift – patience
8th Angel – Cahethel Gift – maturity
9th Angel – Haziel Gift - divine grace
10th Angel Aladiah Gift – rectitude
11th Angel – Laoviah Gift – love
12th Angel – Hahahiah Gift – clairvoyance
13th Angel – Yesalel Gift – friendship
14th Angel – Mebahel Gift – justice
15th Angel – Hariel Gift – purity
16th Angel – Hekamiah Gift – leadership
17th Angel – Lauviah Gift - peace of mind
18th Angel – Caliel Gift – truth
19th Angel – Leuviah Gift – modesty
20th Angel – Pahaliah Gift - intelligence

21st Angel – Nelchael Gift - power

22nd Angel – Ieiaiel Gift – originality

23rd Angel – Melahel Gift – security

24th Angel – Haheuiah Gift – mercy

25th Angel - Nith-Haiah Gift – wisdom

26th Angel – Haaiah Gift – contemplation

27th Angel – Ierathel Gift – freedom

28th Angel – Seheiah Gift – inner strength

29th Angel – Reyel Gift – meditation

30th Angel – Omael Gift – respect

31st Angel – Lecabel - Gift – enlightenment

32nd Angel – Vasahiah Gift – clemency

33rd Angel – Iehuiah Gift – kindness

34th Angel – Lehahiah Gift – affability

35th Angel – Chavakiah Gift – reconciliation

36th Angel – Menadel Gift – prosperity

37th Angel – Aniel Gift - dignity

38th Angel – Haamiah Gift – vision

39th Angel – Rehael Gift – recognition

40th Angel – Ieiazel Gift – writing

41st Angel – Hahahel Gift – fulfillment

42nd Angel – Mikael Gift – diplomacy

43rd Angel – Veuliah Gift – integrity

44th Angel – Yealaiah Gift – memory

45th Angel – Sealiah Gift – humility

46th Angel – Ariel Gift – ingenuity

47th Angel – Asaliah Gift – understanding

48th Angel – Mihael Gift – premonition

49th Angel – Vehuel Gift – generosity

50th Angel – Daniel Gift – inspiration

51st Angel – Hahasiah Gift – creativity

52nd Angel – Imamaiah Gift – security

53rd Angel – Nanael Gift – tranquility
54th Angel – Nithael Gift – stability
55th Angel – Mebahiah Gift – charm
56th Angel – Poiel Gift – prestige
57th Angel – Nemamiah Gift - unconditional love
58th Angel – Ieialel Gift – candor
59th Angel – Harahel Gift – spirituality
60th Angel – Mitzarel Gift – balance
61st Angel - Umabel Gift – sensitivity
62nd Angel - Iah-Hel Gift – honesty
63rd Angel – Anauel Gift – acumen
64th Angel – Mehiel - Gift - willpower
65th Angel – Damabiah Gift – beauty
66th Angel – Manakel Gift – calmness
67th Angel – Ayel Gift – perseverance
68th Angel – Habuhiah Gift - elegance
69th Angel – Rochel Gift – energy
70th Angel – Yabamiah Gift – optimism
71st Angel – Haiaiel Gift – victory
72nd Angel – Mumiah Gift – magic

The Assistance of Angels

You don't only have the support of your guardian angel. All angels are available to help, as long as you ask them.

Know which angels you can ask for help in each situation:

1st Angel – Vehuiah – resolution of difficult situations.

2nd Angel – Jeliel – peace in the home.

3rd Angel – Sitael – in all adversities.

4th Angel – Elemiah – when feeling confused.

5th Angel – Mahasiah – to live in peace.

6th Angel – Lelahel – when you feel that someone means you harm.

7th Angel – Achaiah – when feeling impatient.

8th Angel – Cahethel – for material goods.

9th Angel – Haziel – for the grace of God.

10th Angel – Aladiah - when you are sick or feel victimized by malevolence.

11th Angel – Laoviah – to develop your natural talents.

12th Angel – Hahahiah – when you need to obtain any revelation through dreams.

13th Angel – Yesalel – to protect friendships.

14th Angel – Mebahel – to know the truth.

15th Angel – Hariel – to ask for faith in moments of despair.

16th Angel – Hekamiah – to achieve victory in any matter.

17th Angel – Lauviah – to dispel sadness and sleep well.

18th Angel – Caliel – to confound those who wish you harm.

19th Angel – Leuviah – to increase intelligence and memory.

20th Angel – Pahaliah – to find your vocation.

21st Angel – Nelchael – to protect from slander.

22nd Angel – Ieiaiel – protection on journeys.

23rd Angel – Melahel – protection from assaults.

24th Angel – Haheuiah - to protect exiles, prisoners, and those unjustly condemned.

25th Angel – Nith-Haiah - to discover the truth in spiritual matters.

26th Angel – Haaiah - to win legal cases.

27th Angel – Ierathel - protection in bureaucratic matters.

28th Angel – Seheiah - protection in cases of illness.

29th Angel – Reyel – protection from those who may harm you.

30th Angel – Omael – in moments of despair.

31st Angel – Lecabel – to obtain enlightenment in solving difficult problems.

32nd Angel – Vasahiah – general protection.

33rd Angel – Iehuiah – protection from the envious.

34th Angel – Lehahiah – to live in harmony with others.

35th Angel – Chavakiah – to assist in the reconciliation of couples.

36th Angel – Menadel - to find lost objects.

37th Angel – Aniel – to obtain victories.

38th Angel – Haamiah – to uncover secrets.

39th Angel – Rehael – for your deeds to be recognized by others.

40th Angel – Ieiazel – protects writers and journalists.

41st Angel – Hahahel – against slander.

42nd Angel – Mikael – on journeys.

43rd Angel – Veuliah – to free from addictions and conquer depression.

44th Angel – Yealaiah – assists in legal cases and protects against assaults.

45th Angel – Sealiah – to have hope and overcome pride.

46th Angel – Ariel – to find lost objects and facilitate prophetic dreams.

47th Angel – Asaliah – to achieve goals in any area.

48th Angel – Mihael – to gain inspiration.

49th Angel – Vehuel – facilitates communication with God.

50th Angel – Daniel – decision-making.

51st Angel – Hahasiah – awareness and intelligence.

52nd Angel – Imamaiah – to ward off enemies.

53rd Angel – Nanael – protects teachers and those who work with laws.

54th Angel – Nithael – protects families, businesses, and assists those in need of favors from others.

55th Angel – Mebahiah – protects from people who wish you harm.

56th Angel – Poiel – for obtaining prestige and fortune.

57th Angel – Nemamiah – to fight vices and prosper in all areas.

58th Angel – Ieialel – to overcome sadness.

59th Angel – Harahel – health.

60th Angel – Mitzrael – to be freed from persecution and heal the spirit's ailments.

61st Angel – Umabel – favors studies, especially esoteric ones, and facilitates friendships.

62nd Angel – Iah-Hel – to achieve wisdom and fight violence.

63rd Angel – Anauel – aids in spiritual causes.

64th Angel – Mehiel – protects against traffic accidents, anger, and enmities.

65th Angel – Damabiah – entrepreneurship.

66th Angel – Manakel – helps to calm anger and ward off malice.

67th Angel – Ayel – preservation of material goods.

68th Angel – Habuhiah – health recovery.

69th Angel – Rochel – to achieve fame and fortune.

70th Angel – Yabamiah – protects against bad weather.

71st Angel – Haiaiel – frees from people who wish you harm.

72nd Angel – Mumiah – protects from black magic.

How to Connect with Angels

The most important thing to establish a good connection with angels is the "lightness" of your mind and heart. Hatred, anger, fear, and worries block the communication channels with them. Pray, invoke, meditate, make affirmations... and remember that your guardian angel is always close by, as long as your energy allows it.

The Altar

An altar is a miniature representation of the temple and the universe as a whole, the place where the sacred is reproduced. Any prayer or a simple request are acts of magic that, when possible, should be performed in this place.

Find a space where you feel good and make it your altar.

What you can place on the altar:

• Feathers, flowers, stones, shells, leaves, photos, images... anything that has meaning for you, that reminds you of beautiful moments, that makes you feel connected to the angels and the universe.

Angel Diary

Get a notebook and make it your Angel Diary. In it, you can write everything you think and feel. You can paste images, photos, draw... Make this activity a daily practice, a moment of serenity where you communicate with your angel and free your mind.

Rituals you can practice daily

• **In the morning, upon waking up –**

• Greet your Guardian Angel

- Raise your hands above your head and form a triangle with them.
- Then, place them in front of your chest and greet your angel.
- Take a step forward, open your hands with palms facing up.
- Offer your love and joy and thank them for the help they will provide you throughout the day.
- **Before sleeping –**
- Close your eyes, take a deep breath, relax, and imagine a triangle of white light above you.
- In the centre of that triangle is your guardian angel.
- Feel and visualize them, saying: "Guardian Angel, blessed be for accompanying and loving me. I thank you for today with love."

Angels and Flowers

One way to help your angel get closer to you is to place flowers on your altar, in your home, office... If possible, keep them in the soil, don't cut them. If possible, choose the flowers that correspond to your prince:

Metatron – daisy
Raziel - pansy
Tsaphkiel – violet
Tsadkiel – carnation
Camael – daffodil
Raphael – orchid
Haniel – tulip
Mikael – gladiolus
Gabriel – rose

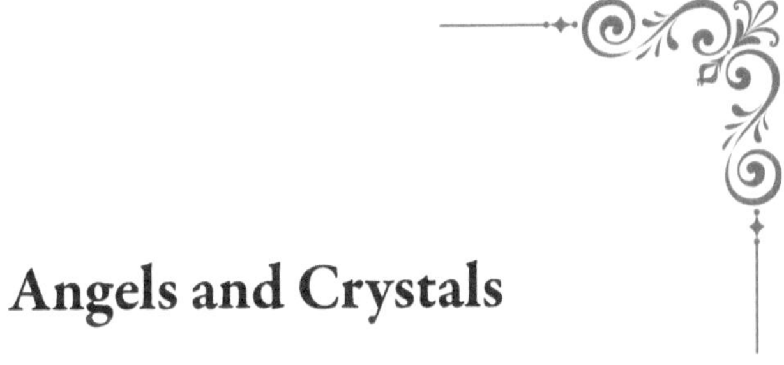

Angels and Crystals

Crystals have the power to balance energies and aid in meditation practice.

Each angelic order corresponds to a crystal. Choose yours according to the order you belong to.

Seraphim – carnelian

Cherubim – topaz

Thrones – jasper

Dominions – chrysolite

Virtues – sapphire

Powers – beryl

Principalities – onyx

Archangels - ruby

Angels - emerald

Crystals need to be cleansed before use.

To cleanse your crystal, you should:

• Place it in a container with water and salt for 24 hours.

• After removing it from the water, without drying it, leave it out under the moonlight for a night.

• The following day, let it be in the sun.

• After completing this cleansing process, consecrate it to your guardian angel and ask them to use it to block all negative energies directed at you.

Now your crystal is ready to be used. You can place it on the altar or carry it with you.

Angels and Essential Oils

Essential oils are a simple and effective way to establish contact with your guardian angel or with any other angel you may need to ask for help.

Before using them, you should focus on the issue or situation you want to resolve and say a prayer. To know which essence to use, consult the following list.

Wormwood – love and sexuality

Acacia – work, business

Rue – cleanses environments of negative energies and spiritually protects

Rosemary – wards off negative thoughts

Lavender – tranquility, positive thoughts

Amber – self-confidence, aphrodisiac

Anise – attracts luck and good energies

Artemisia – stimulates the mind

Vanilla – fights depression

Benzoin – creativity

Coffee – financial prosperity

Chamomile – calming

Cinnamon – aphrodisiac, healing, good vibrations

Camphor – eliminates negative energies

Cedar – harmony, physical energy, divination

Lemon balm – love, relaxation

Fennel - envy

Eucalyptus – renewal of energies

Mint – concentration, decision-making

Orange blossom – love, economic prosperity

Gardenia – peace, love, protection

Ginger – spiritual cleansing, money

Geranium – physical and mental protection

Mint – healing magic, wisdom

Jasmine – physical energy, harmony in relationships

Lavender – good sleep, depression, protection rituals

Lemon – cheerfulness

Lily – love, justice

Honey – overcoming emotional pain

Myrrh – developing intuition

Nutmeg – good luck in business

Frankincense – sorrows, meditation

Pine – prosperity, good luck

Rose – positive energy, love

Sandalwood – intuition, protection, purification

Violet – transmutation of energies

Verbena – love, negative energies

There are various ways to use essential oils, for example:

• As purifiers of negative energies from the body - place a drop of oil on the bath sponge, or use it as a massage oil.

• As purifiers of environments - put a few drops of oil in a litter of boiling water and use it to mop the floor or in a spray bottle. They can also be used pure or in an oil burner. They leave a very pleasant scent in spaces.

Angels and Candles

The flame of a candle symbolizes the light that illuminates the darkness, so lighting a candle with intention is a magical act.

When you wish to light a candle for the angels, you can consecrate it as follows:

• Choose the color of the candle according to what you want to attract (see the next page).

• Use one of the essential oils we recommended in the previous chapter.

• If you want to attract positive energies, rub the candle with the oil from the top (wick) downwards.

• If you want to eliminate negative energies, apply the oil in the opposite direction, from bottom to top. While doing this and when lighting the candle, say your prayer and give thanks.

Pay attention to the message the candle conveys to you (see the following pages).

The Symbolism of Candle Colors

White candle – represents purity and sincerity. Can be used to ward off the contrary spirit and to obtain peace of mind and harmony.

Yellow candle – symbolizes enthusiasm, joy, personal power, and life. Can be used for studies, material goods, and changes.

Red candle – represents courage, passion, strength, and dynamism. Can be used in all cases that require a quick solution.

Blue candle - represents tranquility, understanding, and truth. Can be used for business and profession.

Green candle – symbolizes tranquility and healing. Can be used for health.

Pink candle – represents love and beauty. Can be used for reconciliations, to find love, or in clarifying love doubts.

Purple candle – represents spirituality. Can be used to transmute negative thoughts and to develop intuition.

Messages from Candles

Candle that takes a long time to light – there may be many negative energies around, and the angels have difficulty anchoring. Say a prayer to Archangel Michael.

When the light of the candle takes on shades of blue – it is a sign of the presence of angels.

When the flame forms a spiral – the angels have heard your message, and your desires will be fulfilled.

When the wick splits into two – your request was not clear. The angels are unable to understand. Formulate it again.

When the candle "cries a lot" (small drops fall often) – the angels have difficulty fulfilling what you asked for. It may not be the best for you.

When there is a lot of melted wax in the container in which the candle burned – it is necessary to repeat the prayer more times. Do not give up. Say your prayer daily until the candle's message changes.

Angelic Messages

Whenever you feel the need to "listen" to the angels, you can read an angelic message. You can also do this in the morning when you wake up, to prepare for the new day.

To find out what message the angels are sending you, do the following:

- Roll 2 dice and add the numbers that come up. If you only have one die, roll it twice.
- Read the message corresponding to the number (see the following pages).
- If you prefer, copy the messages onto cards. Shuffle them and draw one.

Messages:

2 – Look at everything with love and you will feel loved.

3- At night, look at the stars and feel that you are part of a fantastic universe.

4- Do not use your words as arrows. Use them to express love.

5- Do not let anger and rage speak for you.

6- If you feel angry, stay silent. Wait for the love of the angels to manifest in you.

7- Be attentive to others. They may need a word of encouragement.

8- Look at each being with love.

9- Do not be afraid. The angels accompany each of your steps.

10- Make this day a magical one.

11- Bring your hope to others and show them that the angels are always with us.

12 – Never forget that you are a special being and the angels love you.

Angelic Visualizations

Visualization is a technique that uses mental images to create what we want to manifest.

By practicing visualization, we combat nervousness and create an environment of peace and harmony that contributes to physical and psychological well-being. This method also awakens intuitive abilities and contributes to the development of spirituality.

How to invoke and visualize angels:

- Sit in a quiet place where you won't be interrupted.
- Close your eyes, slowly.
- Imagine yourself at the centre of a triangle of white light.
- Visualize an angel at each point and tune in to their energy.
- Feel enveloped by the white light that brings you a sense of peace.
- Use the invocations that follow or create your own.
- When invoking, create a clear image in your mind of what you desire. Feel yourself using, being, having... what you ask for.
- At the end, thank the angels and see them rise wrapped in light.

Invocations to attract angels into your life

- I ask for the help of angels at all moments of my life.
- I invoke the angels to guide me towards happiness.
- Angels of light, illuminate my path.
- May the angels bless my choices.
- I invoke the angels to purify my thoughts.
- I invoke the angels to purify my feelings.

Invocations to feel the strength of angels within you

- May the angels envelop and protect me.
- May the angels bless my feelings, my thoughts, and my choices.
- May the angels bless my mind, my body, my spirit, and my emotions.
- May the angels grant me the passion, joy, and courage to express my angelic nature in all my actions.
- May the angels bless me at all moments of my life.

Invocations to feel protected

- I invoke the angels to watch over me at all moments.
- May the angels protect me in all places.

- I invoke the angels to guide my steps away from danger.
- May the light of angels cover me so that no harm comes to me.

Invocations for love relationships

- May the angels bring into my life the relationship that suits me best.
- May the angels bless my life with a loving relationship.
- May my relationship be blessed with the love of the angels.

Invocations to attract prosperity

- May the love of angels help me to prosper.
- I invoke the angels so that my prosperity manifests here and now.
- May the angels guide my steps on the path of prosperity.

Angelic Affirmations

Affirmations, or decrees, are sentences that should be repeated in groups of three or multiples thereof. They can be made at any time and place: while traveling, shopping, at home, on the street... The only thing you need is faith. Angels will add to the power of your words an intensity that will make miracles possible.

Affirmations for:

Feeling the power of angels within you
- My nature is angelic, so angels manifest within me.
- The light of the angels descends upon me.
- Angels guide my life.
- I recognize the angelic potential in others.

Attracting angels into your life
- I open my heart and mind to the guidance of angels.
- My thought is the bridge to the realm of angels.
- I feel the presence of angels at every moment.

Attracting prosperity
- Angels bless my prosperity.
- I know I am protected by angels and will lack nothing.
- I thank the angels for the prosperity they bring me.

Attracting love
- With the blessing of angels, love manifests in my life.
- I trust the angels to guide me on the path of love.

Feeling protected
- I know the angels love and protect me.

- The love of the angels protects my world.
- I feel safe because the angels accompany me.
- I attract the protection of angels in all my actions.
- I thank the angels for their protection.

Attracting angelic healing

- The angels nullify all the pains in my body here and now.
- I attract the healing angels into my life.
- The light of the angels keeps me healthy.
- I thank the angels for their healing.

Angelic Meditations

Learning to meditate with angels will bring many benefits to your life, such as:

- reduced stress and anxiety;
- emotional stability;
- development of creativity, joy, and intuition;
- development of cosmic consciousness.

You can practice meditations in a group or alone, indoors or outdoors.

If you prefer to meditate alone, record the following meditations and use them whenever you feel the desire to connect with the angels.

Guardian Angel Meditation

- Find a quiet place where you feel comfortable.
- Sit down, close your eyes, take a deep breath, and join your hands at chest height.
- Feel your guardian angel approaching you.
- Visualize a white light that envelops you.
- Open your hands, palms up, and place them on your knees.
- Feel the energy of your angel surrounding your hands.
- Send this energy throughout your body.
- Ask your angel to always accompany you.
- Feel the love your angel has for you.
- Embrace yourself.
- Thank your angel for the love in your life.
- Feel your angel's wings touching your arms.

- Slowly, open your eyes, take a deep breath, and thank your angel.

Meditation of the Seven Archangels

- Find a quiet place, outdoors if possible.
- Sit comfortably, take a deep breath, close your eyes, join your hands, and raise them above your head.
- Feel the cosmic energy enveloping you.
- Lower your arms and place your hands in a comfortable position.
- Visualize, in front of you, Archangel Michael.
- Allow yourself to be bathed in the blue light emanating from him.
- Place your hands together near your heart.
- Thank him for his protection.
- Now, gently, turn to your left side.
- Visualize Archangel Jophiel.
- Receive the yellow light emanating from him.
- Thank him for wisdom.
- Visualize Archangel Chamuel now.
- Absorb the pink light he sends you.
- Thank him for love in your life.
- Focus on Archangel Gabriel.
- Allow yourself to be enveloped by his white light.
- Ask him to guide you so you can fulfil your divine plan.
- Give thanks.
- Now, gently turn to your right side.
- Visualize Archangel Raphael.
- Allow yourself to be enveloped by his green light.
- Thank him for health in your life.
- Now direct your gaze towards Archangel Uriel.
- Wrap yourself in the golden light emanating from him.
- Thank him for peace in your life.
- Feel the presence of Archangel Zadkiel.
- Let the violet light he sends transmute your energies.

• Thank him for the tolerance and benevolence you feel towards others.

• Gently, return to the starting position.

• Visualize Archangel Michael again.

• Join your hands and raise them above your head.

• Visualize all the archangels around you.

• Let all the light they send penetrate you.

• Feel peace and love enveloping your entire being.

• Visualize the archangels ascending.

• Thank them for their presence.

• Take a deep breath, lower your arms, extend them forward with palms up.

- Mentally draw a circle around you and visualize it filled with the light and energy you received from the archangels.
- Gently take a deep breath, count to three, and open your eyes.

Meditation of the First Order Angels

- Choose a quiet place where you won't be interrupted.
- If you prefer, put on some relaxing music and light some incense and a candle.
- Stand up, take a deep breath, close your eyes, extend your arms forward with palms up.
- Visualize the Seraphim, Cherubim, and Thrones descending to your side.
- You are at the centre of the triangle they form.
- Sit in a comfortable position.
- Let the light emanating from the angels envelop you.
- Focus on the Seraphim.
- From them, a beam of red light enters you through the third eye chakra.
- Absorb this light and thank them for the abundance in your life.
- Let the red light burn all the insecurity and doubt within you.
- Watch them disappear.
- Look at the Cherubim.
- Visualize a beam of white light emanating from them, entering you through the heart chakra.
- Feel this light burning away your negative karma.
- Give thanks.
- Now, look at the Thrones.
- Visualize a beam of violet light emanating from them, entering you through the solar plexus chakra.
- Feel all your emotional fragility being healed.
- Give thanks.
- Visualize the angels ascending, taking away all your worries with them.

- Give thanks.
- Gently breathe deeply, count to three, and open your eyes.

Meditation of the Second Order Angels

- Find a quiet place outdoors, and lie down.
- Extend your arms along your body, palms facing down.
- Feel your hands receiving energy from the Earth.
- Close your eyes and visualize the Dominations, Powers, and Virtues approaching you.
- Visualize the circle the angels have formed around you.
- Open your arms, turn your palms up, and receive the silver light the Dominations send you.
- Place your arms on your chest, hands joined, and give thanks.
- Open your arms again and visualize the blue light, emanating from the Powers, covering your entire being.
- Place your arms on your chest, join your hands, and give thanks.
- Open your arms once more.
- Absorb the green light from the Virtues.
- Place your arms on your chest, hands joined, and give thanks.
- Stay in position and thank the Dominations for victory in your life; the Powers for guidance they give you, and the Virtues for protection against evil.
- Feel the angels' wings lightly touching your face.
- Wrap yourself in that touch, in that love.
- Stand up and feel the angels circling around you as they ascend, taking away everything you don't want in your life.
- Give thanks.
- Gently breathe deeply, count to three, and open your eyes.

Meditation of the Third Order Angels

- Find a quiet place where you won't be interrupted.
- If you prefer, put on some soft music, and light an incense and a candle.

- Sit comfortably, take a deep breath, and place your hands on your knees, palms up.
- Visualize the Principalities, Archangels, and Angels descending.
- Raise your arms above your head and join your hands.
- Feel the pink light from the Principalities entering you through your fingers.
- Look at them and thank them for the justice they grant you.
- Lower your arms and place your hands joined near your heart.
- Focus on the Archangels.
- Feel all the strength emanating from them.
- Let their blue light form a circle around you.
- Thank them for stability in your life.
- Lower your arms, place your hands on your knees, palms up.
- Watch the Angels.
- Feel a yellow light enveloping you.
- Thank the angels for answering your prayers.
- Feel the rays of pink, blue, and yellow light enveloping your entire being as the Angels ascend.
- Visualize all your worries leaving with them.
- Join your hands and place them near your heart.
- Give thanks.
- Gently breathe deeply, count to three, and open your eyes.

Archangel Zadkiel Meditation

- Find a quiet place, preferably outdoors.
- Sit comfortably and take a deep breath.
- Place your hands on your knees, palms facing up.
- Visualize Archangel Zadkiel.
- Feel the violet light beam emanating from him.
- Feel this light entering you through the crown chakra.
- Now, gently visualize this light descending in a spiral, counter-clockwise.
- See it burning away all the negative beliefs within you.

- Feel the violet light spiral cleansing the third eye chakra; the throat chakra; the heart chakra; the solar plexus chakra; the sacral chakra, and the root chakra.
- Visualize the violet light exiting the root chakra and penetrating the earth.
- Now, visualize the golden light beam that the Archangel sends you.
- Receive it through the crown chakra.
- Let it spiral through all the chakras, clockwise.
- Feel the peace, lightness, confidence, and love that this golden light has brought you.
- Visualize the Archangel ascending.
- Give thanks.
- Gently breathe deeply, count to three, and open your eyes.

Don't miss out!

Visit the website below and you can sign up to receive emails whenever Ana Mafalda Damião publishes a new book. There's no charge and no obligation.

https://books2read.com/r/B-A-KSCEB-FXXYC

BOOKS2READ

Connecting independent readers to independent writers.

Did you love *Angels in Our Life - How to Contact Them and Live in Harmony with the Universe*? Then you should read *The Power of Saint Germain*[1] by Ana Mafalda Damião!

[2]

Dive into a fascinating spiritual journey guided by the sacred traditions surrounding the legendary Master of Transmutation, Saint Germain. This comprehensive guide provides deep insights into the history of Saint Germain, exploring his significance across various spiritual traditions and his enduring legacy.Structured in instructive chapters, the book unveils Saint Germain's teachings, emphasizing spiritual alchemy as a pathway to personal transformation. Readers will be guided through Saint Germain's unique energy, understanding its practical application and intrinsic connection with the universe.The work presents a hands-on approach, demonstrating how to integrate Saint Germain's energy into

1. https://books2read.com/u/mdYQgX

2. https://books2read.com/u/mdYQgX

daily life. Explore guided meditations that open portals to subtle energy, creative visualizations to construct vivid images of transformation, and positive affirmations to tune into the desired energetic frequency.Chapters dedicated to invocation rituals offer insights on creating sacred spaces for deeper connection, while conscious breathing practices teach entering the rhythm of transformation. The book culminates in a powerful gratitude and closing ritual, honoring Saint Germain and concluding the spiritual journey.The conclusion of the book comes full circle, tying together all explored elements, and unveils the inspiring story of Adrian, adding a personal and emotional touch to the narrative. "The Power of Saint Germain" is not just a spiritual guide but a transformative journey offering practical tools for those seeking inner change and spiritual growth.

Also by Ana Mafalda Damião

Aventuras para crianças

Paco: Uma Aventura de Coração

Desenvolvimento Pessoal e Espiritual

Meditação Kind/mindfulness: Programa de 84 dias para mudar a sua
vida

Self-awareness

Therapeutic Writing - the Power of Writing in Personal Transformation

Self-Knowledge and Spiritual Development

Angels in Our Life - How to Contact Them and Live in Harmony with
the Universe

Standalone

Escrita Terapêutica - o poder da escrita na transformação pessoal
Escrever...o quê? 20 + 8 ideias criativas

Escribir... 20 + 8 Ideas Creativas
Anjos na nossa vida - como contactá-los e viver em sintonia com o universo
Oráculo Das Bruxas
Símbolos E Imagens Para Prever O Futuro
Cristalomancia - A Arte Da Adivinhação Com Cristais
Dominomancia - A Arte Da Adivinhação Com O Dominó
Petit Lenormand - Como Interpretar
Oráculo Dos Druidas
O Poder de Saint Germain
Rituais de conexão - Deusas celtas
Connection Rituals – Celtic Goddesses
The Power of Saint Germain
Ten Plagues of Egypt